HOW JELLY ROLL MORTON INVENTED JAZZ

JONAH WINTER

ILLUSTRATED BY

KEITH MALLETT

SQUARE
FISH

ROARING BROOK PRESS

NEW YORK

Here's what could've happened
if you were born a way down south
in New Orleans, in the Land of Dreams
a long, long time ago.

Let's say you had a godmother,
and she put a spell on you
because she was a voodoo queen.

And let's say that when you were a baby,
your godmother brought you to an old saloon
and set you down on top of the bar,
which is not a place for a little baby.

Let's say that some trouble
broke out,
and she got arrested and
thrown in jail,
and you got tossed in
the can as well.

And let's say you just wouldn't stop crying unless all the roughnecks sharing your cell commenced to singing—'cause music was the only thing that calmed you down.

And let's say one day when you were a little older,
you sat right down at a black piano
and you commenced to play,

and you learned to play so well
that soon you were playing with grown-ups,
sneaking out
when the evening sun went down,

playing in bars, surrounded by lowlifes
and dangerous people and folks who loved to
hear you play,

and making more dollars a night
than you knew what to do with.

And let's say you stayed out so late one night
that the night turned into day,

and who should you see coming home
but your great-grandmother
who'd taken you in when your parents had died.
And let's say she asked you where you got your fancy suit.

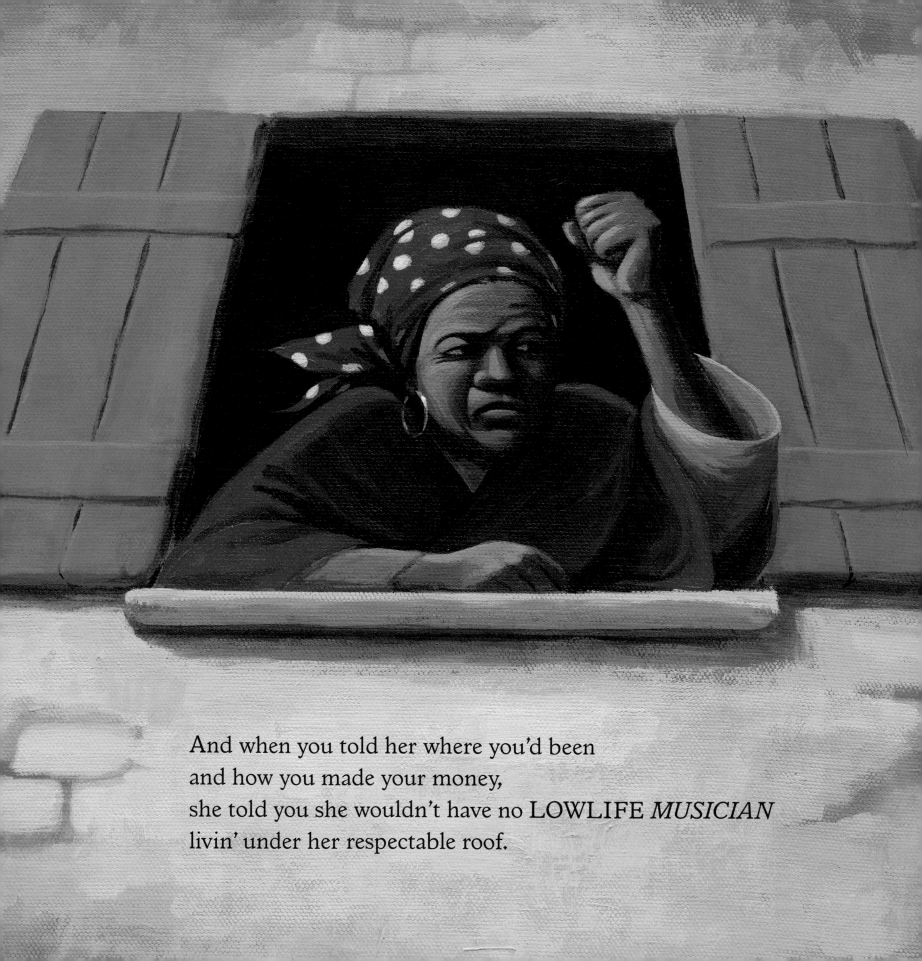

And when you told her where you'd been
and how you made your money,
she told you she wouldn't have no LOWLIFE *MUSICIAN*
livin' under her respectable roof.

And let's say, as you wandered away,
kicked out of your home, still just a kid,
with no place to go,
you started crying so deep inside
that tears would not even fall,

and only one thing,
just one thing in the world,
could make the crying stop:

And this is why
and this is how
a thing called JAZZ got invented
by a man named Jelly Roll Morton.

Leastwise, that's what
I thought I heard Mister Jelly Roll say.
Sing it:

I thought I heard Buddy Bolden say
You're nasty, you're dirty—take it away
You're terrible, you're awful—take it away
I thought I heard him say . . .

I thought I heard Mister Jelly Roll too
Sayin' "I invented jazz in 1902.
It was me who invented jazz—'cause it sure wasn't you."
I thought I heard him too . . .

If you'd been Jelly Roll Morton
you would've known
that the only way to rise up
and fly away
was one piano note at a time.

One piano note at a time
you'd show the folks in New Orleans
who was the best.
You'd show the folks in New Orleans
how it was done—jazz, that is.

What you'd need is a recipe,
as if you were making a great big pot of Creole gumbo stew:

The Recipe for Jazz

You take a town called New Orleans,
You turn up the heat with some African beats,
Throw in some shrimp and crabmeat too,
   sausage and okra, and watch *it* stew.

Spice it up with a dash of Spanish melody
   and island rhythms, Calypso syncopation.

Then stir those reds up with the BLUES
(this ingredient's very important).

Toss in a mess of just messin' around,
Add a pinch of laughter

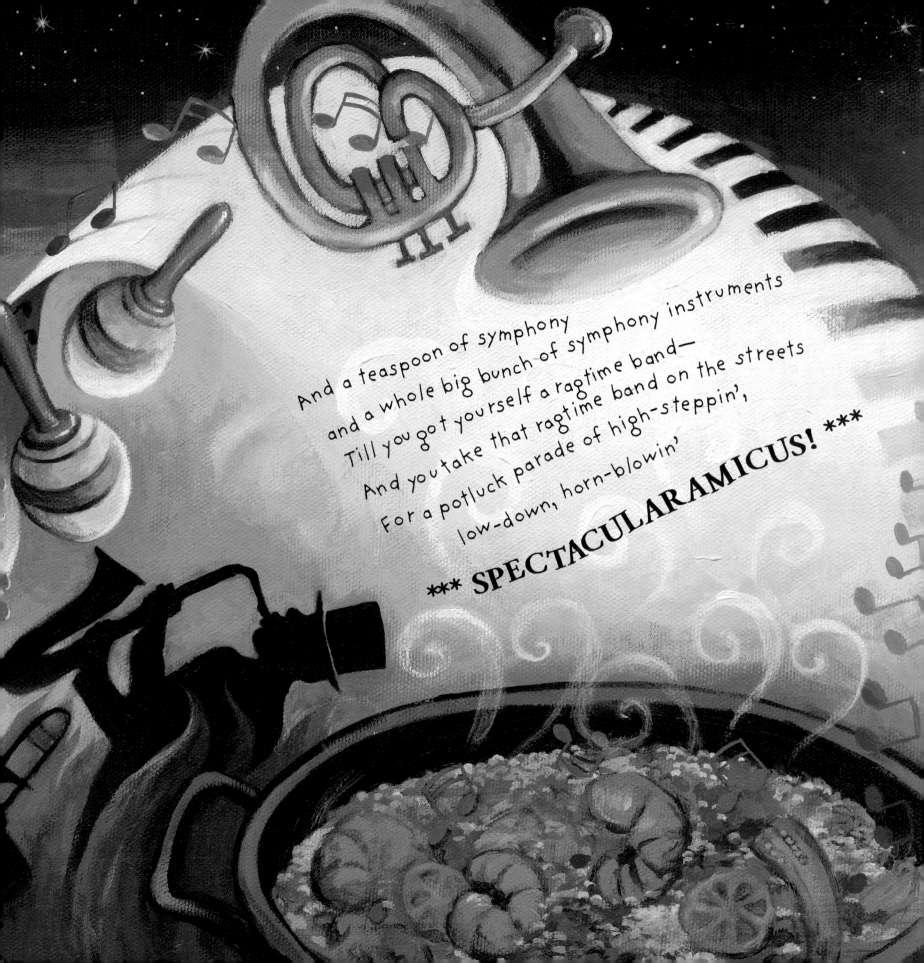

And a teaspoon of symphony
and a whole big bunch of symphony instruments
Till you got yourself a ragtime band—
And you take that ragtime band on the streets
For a potluck parade of high-steppin',
low-down, horn-blowin'

*** SPECTACULARAMICUS! ***

To make this stew, you need a very good cook.
In the darkened corner of the room lit by just a stained-glass lamp,
Jelly Roll Morton begins to play—

And all those different sounds
get blended together
into one sweet and spicy flavor—
smooth, bluesy, something special.

The rose in the bottle,
the moon in the trees,
the twinkling melody
that blows in the breeze:

I'm Alabama bound
I'm Alabama bound
If you like me, sweet baby,
You've got to leave this town . . .

Mister Jelly Roll trucked on down
to Mobile, Alabama—
and trucked on up to Chicago, Illinois ...
and then he commenced to ramble and ramble,
showing each and every poor soul that he met
how jazz was supposed to be played.

And everywhere he went,
it was like he waved a jazzy wand
and cast a voodoo spell
of Jelly Roll magic:
New Orleans, New Orleans, New Orleans . . .

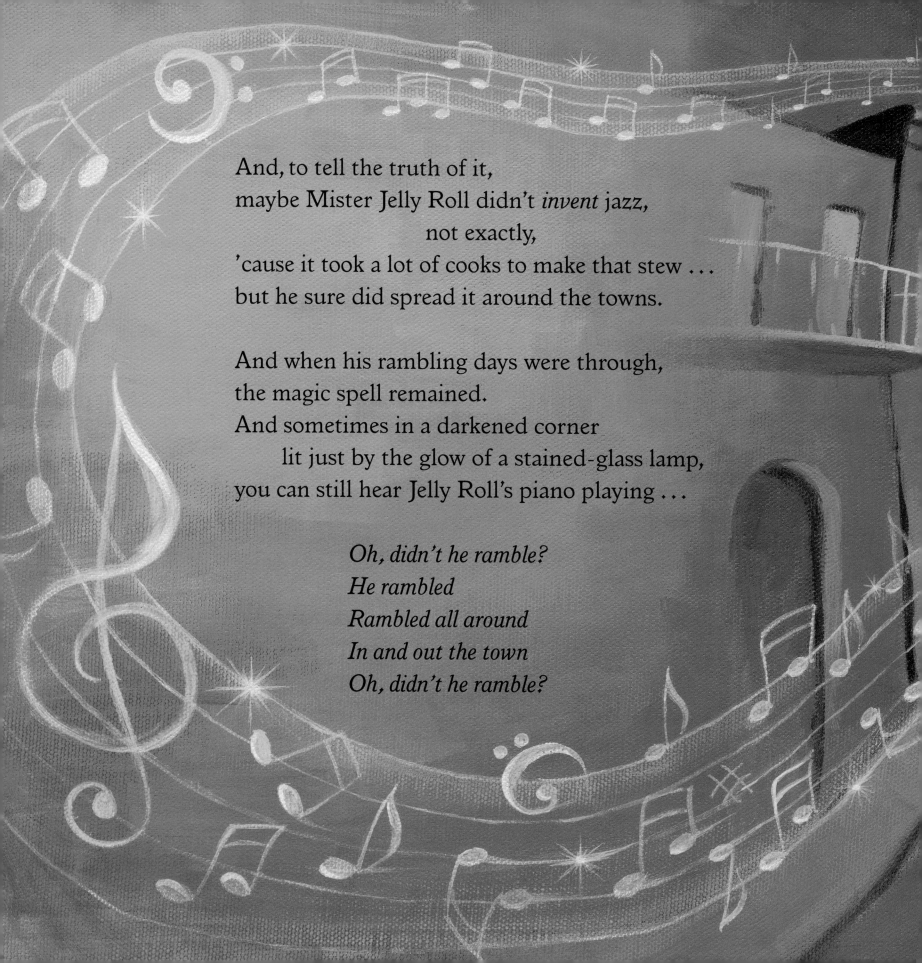

And, to tell the truth of it,
maybe Mister Jelly Roll didn't *invent* jazz,
        not exactly,
'cause it took a lot of cooks to make that stew . . .
but he sure did spread it around the towns.

And when his rambling days were through,
the magic spell remained.
And sometimes in a darkened corner
     lit just by the glow of a stained-glass lamp,
you can still hear Jelly Roll's piano playing . . .

Oh, didn't he ramble?
He rambled
Rambled all around
In and out the town
Oh, didn't he ramble?

HOW JELLY ROLL MORTON (MIGHT HAVE) INVENTED JAZZ

The jazz pioneer known as Jelly Roll Morton was born Ferdinand Joseph La Menthe on October 20, 1890 (or in 1895 . . . or in 1896: nobody seems to know for sure) in New Orleans, Louisiana, the birthplace of jazz and many of the first jazz musicians. New Orleans was an exciting place to be when Jelly Roll was growing up there, and he soaked it all in—while learning, among other instruments, the guitar, the drums, the trombone, and, of course, the piano, the instrument at which he initially earned his fame as the best ragtime and jazz piano player in New Orleans.

One of the most colorful characters in the history of American popular music—with his exquisite suits, his never-ending rambles, his nearly peerless pool playing, and the flashy diamond in his front tooth—Jelly Roll remains both an overlooked and controversial figure, largely due to his manner of tooting his own horn, as it were, as he promoted his own story and its importance to the history of jazz. He claimed not only to have "invented" jazz in 1902 but also to have invented the blues, as well as the words "swing" and "stomp" to describe those particular styles of jazz. He also claimed to be the first person ever to use the word "jazz." Toot! Toot!

However, it can (and has) been argued that Morton tooted his own horn because he never got the recognition he deserved for having played such a significant role in the development of jazz. Even if it cannot be proven that he invented jazz, he clearly was at the very center of the action in New Orleans at about that time—right alongside the legendary Buddy Bolden, whose most famous song is quoted (and added to) in this story. Morton took a lot of different types of music that were happening in New Orleans, as my story suggests, and fused them together into one cohesive way of playing, which he called jazz. Additionally, he was the first musician to publish a jazz composition, "Jelly Roll Blues," in 1915—

which is why he is generally acknowledged as the first jazz composer. What distinguished Morton from his peers was that he wrote and published so many songs and arrangements, and those songs became the standards played by almost everybody in the early days of jazz—and even later, in the 1930s, during the swing era. Sadly, the sheet music companies that published his compositions took most of the money they generated (which was a lot), leaving him penniless at the end of his life. Thankfully, the music historian Alan Lomax sat down with Mr. Jelly Roll a couple of years before he died, recording not just many of Jelly Roll's songs, but also his piano-accompanied narration of the story of early jazz, in which he lovingly presents the styles and names of all the major players in New Orleans, some of which might have otherwise been lost. This set of records is not only a major source of information, it established Morton's importance to music history, and it continues to do so, long after his death on July 10, 1941. Jelly Roll Morton might just have invented jazz . . .

FOR YOUR LISTENING PLEASURE:

Morton, Jelly Roll and Alan Lomax. Jelly Roll Morton: Library of Congress Recordings (Highlights). Rounder Records, 2007.

AND FOR FURTHER INFORMATION ON JELLY ROLL MORTON

(adult biographies: reader discretion advised):

Lomax, Alan. *Mister Jelly Roll: The Fortunes of Jelly Roll Morton, New Orleans Creole and "Inventor of Jazz."* Berkeley, CA: University of California Press, 2001.

Reich, Howard, and William M. Gaines. *Jelly's Blues: The Life, Music, and Redemption of Jelly Roll Morton.* Cambridge, MA: Da Capo Press, 2004.

In loving memory of David McManaway,
who introduced me to Jelly Roll Morton's records when I was a kid.
—J. W.

To Dianne, Christopher, and Pi.
Special thanks to Neal and Jennifer!
—K. M.

Published by Roaring Brook Press
Roaring Brook Press is a division of Holtzbrinck Publishing Holdings Limited Partnership
Paperback published by Square Fish, an imprint of Macmillan Publishing Group, LLC
120 Broadway, New York, NY 10271
mackids.com

Printed in China by RR Donnelley Asia Printing Solutiond Ltd., Dongguan City, Guangdong Province
Square Fish and the Square Fish logo are trademarks of Macmillan and
are used by Roaring Brook Press under license from Macmillan.

Our books may be purchased in bulk for promotional, educational, or business use.
Please contact your local bookseller or the Macmillan Corporate and Premium Sales Department
at (800) 221-7945 ext. 5442 or by email at MacmillanSpecialMarkets@macmillan.com.

Library of Congress Cataloging-in-Publication Data
Winter, Jonah, 1962–
How Jelly Roll Morton invented jazz / Jonah Winter ; illustrated by
Keith Mallett. — First edition.
pages cm
"A Neal Porter Book."
ISBN 978-1-59643-963-4 (hardcover)
1. Morton, Jelly Roll, –1941—Juvenile literature. 2. Jazz
musicians—United States—Biography—Juvenile literature. I. Mallett,
Keith, illustrator. II. Title.
ML3930.M75W56 2015
781.65092—dc23
[B]
2014031487

Originally published in the United States by Neal Porter Books/Roaring Brook Press
First Square Fish edition, 2023
Square Fish logo designed by Filomena Tuosto

Book designed by Jennifer Browne
The art for this book was created using acrylic paint on canvas.

ISBN: 978-1-59643-963-4 (hardcover)

ISBN: 978-1-250-86520-5 (paperback)
1 3 5 7 9 10 8 6 4 2

AR: 4.8